SESAME STREET

Autism Connections

Go with the Flow

All about Flexible Thinking

Leslie Kimmelman

Lerner Publications ◆ Minneapolis

Alongside friends from *Sesame Street*, children will explore how we all experience the world in unique ways—from developing friendships and flexible thinking to how we communicate and receive support. This series celebrates all children, helping young readers and their grown-ups appreciate the amazing qualities in everyone, fostering greater understanding.

Sincerely,
the Editors at Sesame Workshop

Table of Contents

Change Happens!

It's nice to know what's going to happen and when, but sometimes things don't go the way you plan. How do you feel when plans change?

My Granny Bird doesn't feel well. I'm sad because I can't visit her today like we'd planned.

Staying Flexible

Having a routine can make things easier because you know just how your day and night are going to go. You're ready!

It's time for our bubble bath, Rubber Duckie! Then it's time for bed!

Schedules and plans can change. Sometimes you may need to be flexible. Flexible thinking is when you look at situations in different ways.

It rained on our picnic, so we had it inside!

It's OK to feel mad, scared, or disappointed when plans change. Change can be hard.

I can see that you're upset, Julia. Sharing a hug might help.
I love you, Mommy.

You can try belly breathing to help yourself feel better. Put your hands on your tummy. Slowly breathe in through your nose and out through your mouth.

Breathing helps Elmo feel calm. Elmo loves belly breathing!

Remind yourself that there's always next time. Meanwhile, you can get ready for a new adventure!

It's too cold to swim.
But it's a perfect day for flying kites!

Practice being flexible by making small changes first. If your favorite pajamas are in the wash, try wearing your second-favorite pajamas.

Me very flexible.
When me have no more
chocolate chip cookies,
me eat oatmeal cookies
instead!

It's OK to like things to stay the same, but it's important to be flexible. That takes practice!

We can go
with the flow!

Your Turn!

It can be upsetting when things don't go the way you planned. What helps you feel better? Think about what you can try next time!

Blow bubbles

Imagine a favorite quiet spot

Snuggle with someone you love

Dance to your favorite music

Ask a grown-up for help

Glossary

flexible: being able to change plans

plan: a goal to do something

routine: tasks that are done often

schedule: a plan to do things in a certain order

Read More

Bailey, Jenn. *Henry, Like Always*. Chronicle Books, 2023.

Kimmelman, Leslie. *More than Words: The Many Ways We Communicate*. Lerner Publications, 2026.

Schuh, Mari C. *My Life with Autism*. Amicus, 2021.

Index

Photo Acknowledgments

Image credits: fizkes/Getty Images, p. 4; SrdjanPav/Getty Images, p. 6; Milan_Jovic/Getty Images, p. 8; Goran13/Getty Images, p. 10; SDI Productions/Getty Images, p. 12; StockPlanets/Getty Images, p. 14; Elizaveta Starkova/Getty Images, p. 16; Ridofranz/Getty Images, p. 18; Chris Stein/Getty Images, p. 20 (top left); Jonathan Kirn/Getty Images, p. 20 (top middle); vitapix/Getty Images, p. 20 (top right); Phynart Studio/Getty Images, p. 20 (bottom left); Ryan McVay/Getty Images, p. 20 (bottom right).

Lerner Publications Company
An imprint of Lerner Publishing Group, Inc.
241 First Avenue North
Minneapolis, MN 55401 USA

For reading levels and more information, look up this title at www.lernerbooks.com.

Main body text set in Mikado a.
Typeface provided by HvD Fonts.

Editor: Nicole Berglund **Designer:** Mary Ross **Photo Editor:** Nicole Berglund
Lerner team: Martha Kranes

Library of Congress Cataloging-in-Publication Data

The Cataloging-in-Publication Data for *Go With the Flow: All about Flexible Thinking* is on file at the Library of Congress.
ISBN 979-8-7656-8512-9 (lib. bdg.)
ISBN 979-8-3480-2924-1 (pbk.)
ISBN 979-8-7656-9838-9 (epub)

Manufactured in the United States of America
1-1012745-54588-6/27/2025